Atmospheric Embroidery

POEMS

Meena Alexander

TRIQUARTERLY BOOKS/NORTHWESTERN UNIVERSITY PRESS

EVANSTON, ILLINOIS

TriQuarterly Books
Northwestern University Press
www.nupress.northwestern.edu

Printed in the United States of America

10 9 8 7 6 5 4 3 2 1

Library of Congress Cataloging-in-Publication Data
Names: Alexander, Meena, 1951– author.
Title: Atmospheric embroidery : poems / Meena Alexander.
Description: Evanston, Illinois : TriQuarterly Books/Northwestern University Press, 2018. |
    Includes bibliographical references.
Identifiers: LCCN 2018001046| ISBN 9780810137608 (pbk. : alk. paper) |
    ISBN 9780810137615 (ebook)
Classification: LCC PR9499.3.A46 A86 2018 | DDC 811.54—dc23 LC record available at
    https:// lccn.loc.gov/2018001046

Atmospheric Embroidery

Also by Meena Alexander

For
Adam Kuruvilla and Svati Mariam

The awakened, lips parted, the hope, the new ships

—T.S. ELIOT

Working and children & pals are the point of the thing,
for the grand sea awaits us, which will then us toss
& endlessly us undo.

—JOHN BERRYMAN

My last defense
is the present tense.

—GWENDOLYN BROOKS

CONTENTS

One

Aesthetic Knowledge

These are the practices of bodily art—
Burn an almond, collect the soot, mix it with butter.

Enter a cloud
And things are blotted out, ruins restored

So landscape becomes us,
Also an interior space bristling with light.

Have you seen the calendar picture?
Tears from the domes, like droplets of milk

So memories consume a broken mosque.
We are creatures of this world

An invisible grammar holds us in place.
When God shows his face

Even mountains start to blaze.
Burnt rock ground very fine

Becomes surma for the eyes, a divine blessing.
For my Dark Night series I used sumi ink

Culled from the soot of Japanese temples.
For Nur—my Blinding Light series—

Gold leaf pasted on paper,
Utterly fragile.

FOR ZARINA HASHMI

Attar

Soon after we met you set a tiny bottle in my palm.
It had blue whorls and a gold stopper,

Glass blown in the furnaces of Hyderabad.
Open it you whispered,

They call it Attar of the First Rains on Dry Earth:
Pick a piece of wool cotton and pour a drop on it,

Then set it in the broken window frame:
Remember this is the odor of earth and air

This perfume summons souls.

Darling Coffee

The periodic pleasure
    Of small happenings
Is upon us—
    Behind the stalls
At the farmers market
    Snow glinting in heaps,
A cardinal its chest
    Puffed out, bloodshod
Above the piles of awnings,
    Passion's proclivities.
You picking up a sweet potato
    Turning to me —This too?—
Query of tenderness
    Under the blown red wing.
Remember the brazen world?
    Let's find a room
With a window onto elms
    Strung with sunlight,
A café with polished cups,
    Darling Coffee they call it.
May our bed be stoked
    With fresh cut rosemary
And glinting thyme,
    All herbs in due season
Tucked under wild sheets
    Fit for the conjugation of joy.

Little Burnt Holes

Stiff legged, my head and throat so cold, I quit the jury selection room.

I dream of a shop with red velvet curtains where hats the color of bark lie on
the counter,

The hat I want is cut of mink, fit for a brutal season. It has prickles of fur, dirt
colored like the faces of prisoners afloat in the courtroom,

Like the wool Bashō wrapped around his throat when he called on the Lady of
Trees.

All night she sits under a wild flowering tree, ready to judge both the quick and
the dead.

She has a son who breathes fire. Basho whispers to me: In your country they fill
the prisons with dark folk, that's all they care about.

Outside the courtroom, on Center Street, a cold wind rips the scarf off my
head, blinds me.

At night I see the Lady of Trees. She pulls out a handkerchief, makes her fire-
breathing son stop and blow his nose.

Sparks waltz. Her muslin is spotted with little burnt holes.

Debt Ridden

Who are we?

Something was hopping
Up and down in my throat

      O bullfrog

By the stream
Where I was born.

        *

How did we get here?

My mother had a pink
blouse

Over it her sari.

Something

Was torn.

      At first she owed nothing.

Then the sky put paid to us

The wind altered itself
And set us all on fire.

FOR NELL PAINTER

Indian Ocean Blues

L'hibiscus qui n'est pas
autre chose qu'un oeil eclaté.
—AIMÉ CÉSAIRE

SHOOK SILVER

I was a child on the Indian Ocean.
Deck-side we dance in a heat-haze,
Toes squirm under silver wings.
Under burlap someone weeps.

Amma peers out of the porthole
Sari stitched with bits of saffron
Watch out for flying fish,
She cries.

Our boat is bound for Africa.
They have goats and cows just like us,
Also snakes that curl
Under the frangipani tree.

Remember what grandmother said?
If you don't keep that parasol
Over your head
You'll turn into a little black girl.

Where is she now,
Child crossing the livid sea?
Older now,
I must speak to the shadows.

HUMAN GEOGRAPHY

Out of the belly of stone
India pours,
Wild grass is torn
From its roots.

On broken rock
Your face is etched in shadow.
Is this what love does—
Sempiternal marking?

SONG LINES

One sea
Leads to another
(O mirror drunk with salt)
Also to that dreamless sleep

Where all seas start.
On this North American coast
Birch trees swallow the wind
Ranunculus petals tumble

In the heat of spring.
We shut our eyes to the glare
Stumble into the hole
Where Sita lay:

Eye of heaven, earth's soul.
After the trepidation of rocks
After burst blood vessels
Will fields of saxifrage

And self-heal bloom?
Girls gather in sunlight,

Perch on a fault mass
Combing out their hair.

Studio

I was on an island where few birds call.
Old trees swirled in the wind

The door to my studio tore off
Stones struck clouds, church bells echoed

—Earthly unsettlement.
Forced to go on, what did I do?

I pulled down a wall,
Set up another with pasteboard

Tacked a strip of mirror all along the floor
Till white plaster was afloat, gravity unhinged.

The lights I had set up fell to one side,
I stepped through the mirror to touch her—

She was that sort of being, what was the word
You gave me—*sakshi*, yes that.

No one would see her seeing I thought
Without themselves being altered in some way

So in the end she could have a chance
Of being saved from all the body remembers.

I took the face, making it very precise,
Filling in the eyes with several strokes

Reddening under the lids—fire turned to blood,
Each element as the Gnostics tell us

Resolved into its own roots.
The neck of course is simple and straight.

She is in a white dress as usual,
A child whose mother

Takes pleasure in dressing her well.
In the end my hands were pocked

And bruised with paint
And when I lifted them off the canvas

I felt something warm,
Very like torn skin fluttering off.

FOR CECILIA EDEFALK

Net Work

She cut off all her hair,
Scampered down a staircase, skinned her knees.
Years later she pinched herself awake
Hearing words in a foreign language,
Books she longed to read, smudged with sunlight.
Broadway and 113th Street she whispered to herself
The sheer delight of walking a city street couldn't be rivaled.

Her preferred method of work:
On an iPad, sitting in a sidewalk café.
What she could not bear to think
She wrote. One by one she composed her lines
She numbered each with finicky care, struck—Send.
Her hope was that her sentences would net a quicksilver "I"
Swimming in ether.

1. *When we landed there were three of us.*
2. *All our worldly goods were packed in a holdall.*
3. *Pots and pans cleaned with well water. And that was that.*
4. *Is this a Third World country or is it not? Mother mumbled into her sari.*
5. *Trouser wearing women were an abomination, this Father knew.*
6. *I did algorithms, hoping long skirts would not trap.*
7. *The river's so close, can I swim to another shore?*

Bright Passage

Grandmother's sari, freckles of gold poured into silk,
Koil's cry, scrap of khadi grandfather spun,
I pluck all this from my suitcase, its buckles dented, zipper torn.
Also pictures pressed into an album: parents by a rosebush,
Ancestors startled in sepia, eyes wide open—
Why have you brought us here?

Mist soars on the river, my door splits free of its hinges:
My children's children, and those I will never see—generations swarm in me,
Born to this North American soil, dreamers in a new world.
I must pass through that rocking doorway,
Figure out words, clean minted, untranslatable—O body, bright passage—
Already in the trees, finches are calling, warbling my name.

Blues

Blood droppings on sand,
The sheep are leaping into water—what music here?

As the rain falls
As the rain falls in Long Beach, his voice fills the room.

Saraswati of the broken seawall
Saraswati of raw eggs and slipshod girls

Goddess of the feverish tide
And storm-drunk saxophones

Speak to me.

Two

Indian Ocean Blues

FERMATA

He rode the waves,
Jungli man with bits of silver on his eyes
Head poked with horns, his arms were cut.

Bras-Coupé!
I yelled. All amma could see
Buried under a blanket as waves rose
Was my black tousled head.

In dreams I was a child
With hands lopped off.
What had I done?
No one knew.

As the steamer floated to Aden
They shot gulls
From the cliffs
Those Englishmen—

Their bullets flew,
Struck a boy
Herding goats on high
Rocks by the reddening sea.

UDISTHANAM

Piercings of sense,
Notes lashing time
Ecstatic self hidden
In the ship's hold

"I" legible
Solely in darkness:
Shot flames,
Anchorage of divinity.

On the South Indian coast
In eighth century heat
Tiruvalla copper-plate
Marked the morning hour

Before the sea clamored
And the shadow of the body
Lay twelve feet longer
Than Sita herself,

Littoral burning
With sacred fires—passage
To a kingdom beyond
The pipal trees.

Where are those refugees
Amma did not want me to see,
Gunny sacks and torn saris
Stitched together with cord?

Breath of my breath, bone
Of my bone, dark god
Of the Nilgiris,
Who will grant them passage?

Phillis Wheatley Suite

STICKS AND STONES

Thrust into the maw (Where was your mother?)
Altered in the stench, in the bog down there—

Afterwards to pour yourself
Into words, into that strangest lyre, strings sucked

Tongue torqued, fierce filigree
God, Master, White, Ethiop, words sentient, insolvent.

SLOW BURN

Girl child, named for a slow vessel
Pass through fear into that azure ring

Where ghosts swim.
Write to the Generalissimo of the Armies of North America

The way you were sure he wished to be addressed,
A letter with a poem stitched to it.

Think of troops half starved in winter
Their backs trembling against basalt

In a place of bedrock and river glow,
Washington Heights as now it is known.

As you write, feel a swan's feather
Brushing icicles off your back,

A coarse blanket that covered your nakedness
When they bought you, slipping off;

Your skin blue, ablaze
In a place where you have nothing left to lose.

Harlem Cleopatra

Cleopatra in dark glasses turns a corner
And comes upon MORRIS GITTELL INSURANCE BROKER

She hides behind a pillar
So he will not see her, the child loitering, close to the sign—

We Help You in Obtaining Your Birth Certificate
Especially If You Were Born in the South.

Why is the boy standing there?
Dressed in his hooded sweatshirt

He ducks his head, murmuring yes, yes,
To that other life, not yet come.

Something floats between her skin
And glass, a cluster of risky hieroglyphs—

Rare Almagest, the mysteries of birth and death
Cut from a platinum bath.

Haunted by light a man stood for hours,
Hands soaked, getting it just right.

She watched him with his camera,
Scarf to his throat, lens glinting.

Dear Damage—she writes in her own head—
My soul knows rivers.

She adjusts her glasses, watches the boy
Naked, gleaming with Nile water,

Torn apart, Osiris, all his flesh thrown
Into the pitch drunk Mississippi,

Then cheeks stung with rock rose and eglantine,
Miraculously whole, racing through plots

Of bullwhips and manacles.
Now she sees him step out of the C train,

Strolling up Sugar Hill in dun colored flannels,
Houndstooth jacket slung over his shoulder,

A grown man, hair white, smoldering in sunlight:
The children of Gaza sing in his veins.

I cannot get him out of my mind, she whispers
To no one in particular.

He is that lad and he is Osiris,
Come to live in me, part of the stumbling glory of things.

(INSPIRED BY A PHOTOGRAPH BY ROY DECARAVA)

Magnificat

On the road near the hospital
A plum tree points to Krakatoa and her plumage

The skies Munch painted athwart an open mouth
Are molten still, the tint of ripe plums.

The radiologist a young thing quips—New kind of tattoo—
Marks initials on my breast

A man in a mask scrawls *X* under that
His eyes dark with volcanic mist

(The one in Iceland,
Sooting up airspace, grounding planes).

My niece said—As Sarah died, we sat up all night,
Five women massaging her hands, her feet.

Afterwards our eyes were like that:
My niece forced her eyes wider with her fingers

Pupils roared. ROYGBIV.
All objects emit radiation—*My soul doth magnify the Lord*

In the hospital window leaves burn—
The color of Mary's cheeks when the angel tore in with his trumpet.

You are quite well now, quite well really, voices chime.
A rougher voice: We must take care of the hole

In the ozone layer before more of us fall through.
Some of us become death's midwives.

Question: What holds up the rainbow?
Answer: Only a little fountain of wind.

The Journey

I was blindfolded and had only the mercy of the sea
(And sprigs of jasmine in my arms).

The journey was awkward: lines blown inward, syllables askew.
Gulls nestled in torn pages.

There were many languages flowing in the fountain
In spite of certain confusion I decided not to stay thirsty.

When we got to that country, a war was going on
A mound of stones grew outside our window frame.

I was five years old and tried to understand what was happening.
My soul ran away with me.

Forests with branches torn off, mouths that split open into my mouth,
Eyes that mirrored mine, ears torn off, few birds warbling.

Close at hand, afloat on water, a tall cliff scarred with glyphs,
Visionary want, attuned to nature's substances.

Rock and ruin, pathways of salt, scents of crushed jasmine,
Returning me to what I cannot bear to remember.

Darfur Poems

On a cloud I saw a child

—WILLIAM BLAKE

SAND MUSIC

The wind is blurring our faces
We do not know who we are or what songs we might sing.
A stranger enters the village, lets go his horse.
A woman drags a cart filled with pots and pans
Pulling the sky behind her.
When I was a young girl I saw nothing,
My skin set fire to everything.
A tethered horse is pecked to death by songbirds.
In Muhagiriya everything's laid out
As if in a Japanese garden, the sort one dreams of—
Circles of sand, beaten rocks, tree stumps
Tilting into blue. A child's elbow pokes out of a well.
In a mosque, men kneeling, five beheaded.
And the daughters of music brought low.

IN OUR LIFETIME

Flushed by the rose of flesh
Pierced by barbed wire, a wound that will not heal.
The iron of attachment cuts
What we take for ourselves, ways of living
That will not last for very long, untenable, yes.
A boy moves on the plain, his goats beside him.
Trying to find his way through clouds of dust—
Haskanita, where children rushed by men
On horseback discover the guns temerity,
Where stars startle themselves in broken water
And the boy with his goats, trying to turn home
Remembers what his father never told him—
Open your legs wide, run
Not *those staggering towards slaughter.*

GREEN LEAVES OF EL FASHER

Everything that's real turns to sun
Stones, trees, the jeeps they came in, those men.
In Jebel Marra, the leaves are very green.
Here, in El Fasher too.
I am singing, stones fill with music.
Do not touch my hair, I cried. They forced me
To uncover my head then beat me when my veil slipped,
Not the pink one I am wearing now, with stripes—this
My aunt gave me. I am not an animal,
They are more free, birds in the tree, horses too.
I am your language, do not cover me.
I am burning in what you take to be the present tense.
We are the letters *alif, ba, taa, mim*—
What the sun makes as it spins a nest of fire.

NURREDIN

A garden bright with fruit trees,
Each tree, in its own shadow, singing.
Above our house, a cloud of locusts stinging.

Mother lay not moving, out of her throat
A black river. I saw a man with a gun
In his mouth, he was trying to eat it.

From the cloud-ship Antonov drops fell

We ran to the wadi, many people came.
Creatures too, camels, dogs, cats with no fur

Birds with torn wings.
I curled up in the wadi house,
Hungry, with bones and ash to stay.

Remember me, Nurredin

My name means light of day.

LAST COLORS

In another country, in a tent under a tree,
A child sets paper to rock,
Picks up a crayon, draws a woman with a scarlet face,
Arms outstretched, body flung into blue.

(*Hashsha*—to beat down leaves from a tree.)

The child draws an armored vehicle, guns sticking out
Purple flames, orange and yellow jabbing,
A bounty of crayons, a hut burst into glory.

(*Yatima*—to be an orphan, the verb intransitive.)

The child draws what's near at hand and common
Not what's far away—not the ghost house
In Khartoum where a father lies
Whose hands and ears are torn.

(*Idhash-shamsukuwwirat*—so the sun is overthrown.)

Child's Notebook

Preserved in the torn pages
Of a notebook (double leaved)
The houses start up.
Everything is emptied out.
Prickly pear, race around it
Ravaged—blunt
Dashes of red
Men and women mingle:
A cactus bud
A bomb, a house, a haven
Horsemen, an unbegotten
Species, a desolation.

On the facing page
A giant bird, an ostrich
Thighs pink, head tiny, staring.
A gunship clay colored, fires:
(Holes in paper
A pencil poked through).
Blue wings boil in sand
Where stick houses stand
And souls float, brighter than air
As a child, seated on a stone
Reaches out her hand to draw.

There She Stands

On a cloud,
A child, arms splayed.

Beneath her, a field.
Red trees

With creatures clinging on—
Cat dog goat mother father too.

How are they all going to live?
A hard wind blows.

The camels don't get it,
They keep coming back.

One of them has a new
Hump—guns poke through.

Close to the child
A thorn bush burns:

Celestial now
Witnessing damage.

Fragment in Praise of the Book

Book with the word for love
In all the languages that flow through me
Book made of leaves from a mango tree
Book of rice paper tossed by monsoon winds
Book of pearls from grandmother's wrist
Book of bottle glass rinsed by the sea
—Book of the illiterate heart—
Book of alphabets burnt so the truth can be told
Book of fire on Al-Mutanabbi Street
Book for a child who wakes to smoldering ash
Book of singing grief
Book of reeds vanishing as light pours through.

Night Theater

Snails circle
A shed where a child was born.

She bled into straw—
Who can write this?

Under Arcturus
Rubble of light:

We have no words
For what is happening—

Still language endures
Celan said

As he stood in a torn
Green coat

Shivering a little,
In a night theater, in Bremen.

Chilika Lake

The prose of the world is taunting me,
The lonely girls are blossoming too fast
In their fuming silks and chiffons,
Some will float in the warmth of lake water
Gone to hell for love, nothing but.
I kneel in a jungle of sweat, ruin of old bone
I salt cucumber and set it at my mother's feet
Already she is ninety years old.
In the mirror she sees specks of lava.
The village where she was born is deserted—
Just a raw road, counterfeit bills, carnage of crows
Hurried betrothals behind cheap mauve curtains
As stray dogs turn into messengers of Bacchus.
Sometimes I think the past is a boom-or-bust theater
With backlit clouds, baffling us,
With wild auteurs, amateurs of skin,
Festoons of words no one believes.
Still the planet's heat is too much to bear
When life ends who will be with her?
Chilika Lake is nothing but a dream.

Dreaming in Shimla—Letter to My Mother

Grandmother died with absolutely no warning, left you a raw girl clad in cotton, barely sixteen, weeping into your own sleeve.

No mother and a father who did not really care for you—forced to walk on eggshells

Rub-a-dub-dub of wretched want and need.

Stony tutelage.

In Grandmother's diary, in her firm rounded hand, she wonders aloud
what to pay the dhobi, the woman who pounds rice, the man who harvests
pepper from the twisted vines.

Must she burn all her silks in the nationalist bonfire

Can she keep a few?

*

Far to the north in the half-timbered stables where I lodge, I listen for the
snort of horses, crude rub of saddle against flank,
Englishmen with polished boots yelling for valet, butler, chowkidar.

As hailstones strike the roof I crouch on the floor, set buckets under all the
spots where plaster darkens and water drips.

Grandmother's diary curls in a leather suitcase thrust under the bed.

Come daylight I hear charred whispers

The centuries doubling back, feverish, irresolute—

Girls bearing firewood for the fretted furnaces of lords and ladies, ashen women with their makeshift canes

Bodies bent in a hoarse wind that rattles bridge and bay window, spews dirt onto pillar and polished marble

The furious wealth of empire—

Then come quick hooves of horses in caracole forcing me to shut my eyes and dream

Hard dreaming, mother, on a cold mountain slope.

*

Children from a little school beat drums, chant their lessons. What do they learn?

A brown bird cries out from the deodar trees. It has no name.
It makes warbling cries I cannot catch. Nothing to punctuate those sounds except wild air.

The heart's illiterate, dear mother.

No reading or writing in those bloody clavicles.
Only whispered words, illegible sentences

And all the marks the body bears—
Violent, ecstatic, lingering.

Game of Ghosts

No water in the fountain.
The garden of consolations is at hand.

Twin monkeys pick at the edge of the lawn
Who knew they ate grass?

Sunlight, a mauve hibiscus consumes itself,
Bare stalks flash.

Someone is playing tennis on Lord Dufferin's court
He puts us all to shame—

He comes closer and closer the beautiful boy
He has no toes.

Three

Atmospheric Embroidery

Wads of ice cream glisten on Route 6.
We stroll into summer, thoughts thrust into a bramble

Oriental bittersweet pocking the hedges,
Fists in pockets, lemonade dripping from a child's hem.

In Boetti's embroidery, in his mapping of the world
Everything is cut and coupled,

Occult ordering—silk and painted steel
Sun and electric moon, butterfly and naked man.

In *The Thousand Longest Rivers*
The Nile is the hardest water

Then comes the Mississippi–Missouri.
Once we lived by brilliant waters

Suffered the trees soft babble,
Fissures in magma.

Already it's August—
Season of snipers in the heartland

Season of coastlines slit by lightning
And smashed bouquets of the salt spray rose.

Now I think it's a miracle we were able, ever
To put one foot in front of the other and keep on walking.

Univocity

Word over all, beautiful as the sky!

—WALT WHITMAN

PROVINCETOWN BY THE SEA

As August fades I pedal hard.
At Angel Food I pick up Portuguese fig cake,

Almonds cut and buried in speckled dark,
Pinpricks of sweetness bound in Saran Wrap.

In the High Middle Ages
Theologians mused how angels pranced

On the head of a pin,
How the spirit could spin cocoons of flesh,

Whether a body could be in two places at once.
Almost always

I am in two places at once,
Sometimes in three.

Free me weep me Motherwell by the sea,
Night waves succor you.

You knelt on the floor by the canvas, thrust hard:
I made the painted spray

With such physical force
That the strong rag paper split.

SCRIM-SCRAM OF MUSIC

How her wrists hurt when she piano played.
He was new in town, the English doctor

In pith helmet and crisp white shirt.
A brand-new cure—he pricked her hard.

Drops of gold made her bones boil,
Tongue flower with blisters.

She was dead in a day
One month short of fifty.

Moonlight, darkening storm
Dove sta memoria.

I never knew my mother's mother.
In her diaries the recipe for mutton curry

(Five cloves of garlic, a fistful of green chilies)
Sits athwart Gandhi's injunction to spin—

I have laid out my khadi, washed and ironed it.
Tomorrow when I wear it, the sky will be blue.

Nothing known—
The curse and blessing

Torn rag I pack around the wound,
Curbing the flow that could kill.

TORN BRANCHES

Grandfather lies in wait for me.
I cannot flee.

My voice is young and burnt
My voice is a bramble berry squashed on stone.

All afternoon I lay curled in a hole
In the bamboo grove where cobras rove.

No one knew.
Rove—how did I learn that verb?

From my Scottish tutor—
She rapped my knuckles hard.

A swan in a bag, worth two in the lake.

A stitch in time saves nine.

She taught me some such things.
Who will bring me sweetmeats

Swirl henna on my palms?
Who stokes sugarcane with kerosene

Binds cords of broken rope?
Dark sisters in the sky, their wings are torn.

They have stumps for wrists.
They sing hosannas to our Lord.

ARS POETICA

By the crook of my knees
I hang in a mango tree.

The leaves are very green.
I slip a finger under my skirt,

I touch the bark of the tree with wetness.

I write on knobbly bark.

A red ant crawls on my skin.
I turn my face to the sky.

The blue is splattered with white
I write the sky.

The blue is cut with reddish flecks.
From a great distance, they are calling me

I am in the green tree,
They keep calling my name.

When I hear their voices
My finger threatens to catch fire.

LINES WITH RED ANTS

Some things have holes in them
Leaves on the mango tree

When sparks fly through.
I have a hole in between my legs

I pick red ants off the tree,

I let them crawl over me

Fire blossoms where they bit.
I liked it when the red ants bit.

BATHTUB BLUES

At the edge of eleven a child
Crouches in a bathtub

Silver scissors in hand,
Skin trembling under metal

The first materiality is all we have.
Duns Scotus knew this.

The child meets him in the dark,
His loincloth was made of glass.

She whispers words she learnt by heart.
O the mind, mind has mountains; cliffs of fall.

He forced her to see
Things that beggar speech

(Will strips of chiffon wrap around bone?)
Doctor Subtilis, please save me!

THIS IS NOT A DREAM

Someone stoops at the edge of a pit
The pit is covered with sticks and leaves

In the park the air is heavy
In the park the air is indigo.

Matchstick blue
The scrawl of circling birds.

The snare of love—
Impossible to crawl through.

BLACK SAND AT THE EDGE OF THE SEA

Soon I will be given to earth,
Folded in a death squat

Together with pig marrow,
Swan's down, thread leaved sundew,

Pitchblende sucking bones in.
Where is grandfather now?

My friend says think of old Walt
Bent over his dead enemy—

Touching lips to encoffined flesh.
So where do they live

The twin sisters Night and Death?
Will they wash the ground clean?

Indian Ocean Blues

INWOOD SITA

Sita bathed in sand.
By wildwort
And willow herb
Fire starts—

Dry ground cracks,
Swallows her whole.
Sita-found-in-a-field
Fled to Inwood.

Rama cast her out,
Lava storms cooled her
Dirt cloaked her,
A shimmering stole.

Days later, on Dyckman Street
As cobbles crack
She slips into a manhole,
Waves at me.

TARAWAD

You find this hard to believe:
I am a creature of house and home
Bound by a cord of blood—
Wild grasses blazed, nettles turned

Their stalks to the setting sun.
I was born to a house with red tiled roof,
Courtyard where sunbirds drew
Glittering beaks across mulberry bark,

Pond where koi crawled
Then shot into light, circling
The mouth of the lotus bloom.
House of mist and stone,

Unseen umbilicus
That tethered me
Even as the ocean
Swept on and on.

Going, going, gone!

Someone banged the gavel.
Hearing the house was sold
She lay down in the mango grove
And stopped her eyes with stones,

Crazy girl, inconsolable!
Where is she now?
Where is the path where laburnum
Dropped its liquid gold,

Casuarinas flashed green needles into flints?
Jamun and jacaranda trees chopped.
Down into the hole
He went the priest in white robes

Singing praises
To the Lamb of God.
Tor of fragments,
Blunt pinnacle of longing

What becomes of houses torn down?
In the room where she slept
Milk trickles
Syllables swarm, lacking a script

Doorjamb stuck to emptiness

Threshold split from walls.

SYNCOPATION

Be fearless with density
You whisper to me
It too is an accumulation of longing,
A sideways swipe at the stars.

We are leaving one
Language for the other,
Always and ever—
What crossing enjoins.

Waves of hope,
Bitter notes plucked from sea foam,
Beauty's tribulation,
Virus of the possible,

Arco of love
Slow fingering of desire,
Our saris packed
Into one battered suitcase

Old leather rinsed
With moonlight as underwater
Continental plates clash
And on a sodden deck

He rises,
Cloaked in amaranth petals
A big man, his wounds
Molten.

What spills
From his lips?

Can Krishna
Hear him calling?

PITCHING A TENT

Where the ground shakes
I set my tent.
We cannot know ourselves ever.
I write this on your sleeve,

Fold the cotton over.
Sweet sunlight—

What swans found
In their last flight.

Dwelling

Look I have set my house on fire!

—KABIR

I used to live in the Bronx. One night I covered my manuscript in a woolen shawl and carried it to the incinerator. I opened the metal bin, shoved it in. The shawl had flowers and bird beaks embroidered on the border.

I could hear crackling when the edges caught fire.

*

A friend came for dinner. He entered our apartment at the edge of Fort Washington Avenue, he stared at the black trees outside the window. He settled into the couch.

Two months earlier his wife had killed herself plunging a knife into her chest. She was lying on the bed when he entered.

There was blood everywhere. I got a new bed. I thought he was going to choke, the way he said it. He pointed to his book bag—green with blue straps, a meager thing.

I go from house to house. I live out of that, he said.

*

I make the jitney to Mattituck. K. and I have been friends for thirty years. Her house is brand-new. On the lawn the *swit-swit* of tiny earth creatures,

Bustle of birds, insects rubbing against grass blades, swarm of crickets. We spill over our shadows, traipse to the pool.

Resist the temptation to look in.

*

K. introduces me to Barthes's *Mourning Diary*. He wrote it after his mother died. My own mother lies in hospital. She has a lump on her neck. No one knows the cause.

The windows have green shutters. The nurses keep coming in. What do they think I am? Amma whispers on the phone. That night I see a nurse all veiled in white.

She has no eyes.

*

In Mattituck, cocooned in sheets, I see the Untouchable man who chopped wood, then begged for silver. He wants to put the coins on his own eyes when he dies, Grandfather said—

Untouchable means someone whose touch pollutes you. Even the shadow can do this. They used to beat drums to warn people they were coming close. This was in the house of my childhood, the house with the courtyard where the mulberry tree bloomed.

He must hate us for living here, for making him chop wood, I said to grandfather. The wind rose in the mango trees and whipped against the wood stumps piled by the well side.

Some of the stumps were tied with black cord.

*

The path of social reform like the path to heaven (at any rate in India) is strewn with many difficulties, Ambedkar wrote. *The Untouchable was required to have a black thread either on his wrist or around his neck,*

As a sign or a mark to prevent the Hindus from getting themselves polluted.

*

So it was that we dwelt in the house. A verb deliberately archaic (Old English *dwellan—to lead or go astray, hinder, delay, stun*). Five decades after Grandfather's death, four years ago to this date, the house was sold to a distant cousin. Gutted, a deliberate ruin.

The land is used for a block of luxury flats, complete with swimming pool.

*

I crouch in front of a light box, out of it comes a sonic scape, pitched higher than I can bear. In a back room of MOMA fluted cries of forest birds, some already extinct.

Childhood come back, pure black happiness. My shadow and I sit weeping.

Bird sounds trapped in a forest, magnified by machines, else inaudible. The forest in the mind's space, an openness sunk in darkness.

What does it mean to conjugate joy?

Elsewhere air axed, trees burnt, ground clawed apart for bauxite.

*

K. tells me that the lines I hope to write about the house of my childhood, destroyed now, could make a poem. It's your voice she says. I wish I could believe her. I make a show of thrusting out with my elbows

As babies do, wet and bloodied, after being born.

*

Nothing is nowhere. This rings in my ear—line from a handbook for teaching English in Dubai .(I find the book shoved into the seat pocket of a plane circling above Kochi.)

I keep flying says the stewardess who wears a blue hat—I could not bear to stop.

The past returns as penitence—what might this mean?

*

I see my old friend in West Side Market, by the stall of tomatoes. He waves at me. He has his backpack. Is he still going from house to house? I cannot ask him that.

In my notebook lines from Barthes copied in over a month ago—*Since maman's death, despite—or because of it—a strenuous effort to set up a grand project of writing, a gradual alteration of confidence in myself—*

In what I write.

*

Mother takes leave of her mind. She knows Grandfather has come to get her. He's walking by the well side, she cries on the telephone.

A nurse pushes open the door to my mother's hospital room.

She has no eyes.

*

*As soon as someone dies, frenzied construction of the
future (shifting furniture, etc.): futuromania.*

*

Once I had a manuscript, I say to Kimiko. I will dwell in it. I wrapped it in an
embroidered cloth, bore it, ever so tenderly to the incinerator chute.

Forever after a feeling of flesh bathed in flame.

*

Flight of geese over her house. Red maples quivering. I do not find a word for
the sound the leaves make. They fly from the fields to the lake K. says.

Close, see how close?

FOR KIMIKO HAHN

Fragments of an Inexistent Whole

Syllables sieved through floating gates,
Metal clack of printer

Mortal rendition, Fortran—
The future coming closer and closer

House of broken dishes / by the sea / using electricity

Black flash, strange as any *me* I might claim

The already gone, its music barely audible
00–111—000 cut and sizzling, swiveling repetitions

The mind falling from itself, into no *where*.
The desire for place not to be denied

What touch affords us, sempiternal hold.

*

Imagine a woman with a veil over her head,
Black cotton or muslin

Of the sort that my grandmother wore, the edge of her sari
As she sat under the sun, by the well side.

Already the veil covers the garden
Mango trees split into the shape of harps.

*

The artist decides on materials, timber, tar, tumbleweed,
Then light source—natural, electric, strobe, that sort of thing

She decides on location—
A bracelet, a brandishing of space

Scores for a masked ball, the self and its others
Clinging close, hips grinding, a distinct congress

Precise rendering of rhyme or its uncoupling
Underwater copulation = syllabic sense.

The artist decides on persons—girls with jump ropes
Boys whistling in the sunlight by hydrants gushing

Hot metals, the planet soaked in ether,
A scholar blinded by footnotes, scores of them,

Men and women, faceless now, joyful and inconsolable
Veritable census of the dead.

                                    *

House of Dust / on open ground / lit by natural light
Is that where I belong?

Lord have mercy!
Grandmother cried, when I was born

This child will wander all her life.
Grandfather tossed in a match

The bush filled with smoke, gooseberry bush—
With freckled leaves

—Tat tvam asi—
The deliverance of Sanskrit

What I learnt without knowing that I did,
Grammar of redemption

Sucked from fiery space
As Grandmother's hands turn to dirt

The sky—cerulean blue

Sheer aftermath.

(INSPIRED BY ALISON KNOWLES'S COMPUTER-
GENERATED POEM "THE HOUSE OF DUST")

Death of a Young Dalit

Trees are hoisted by their own shadows
Air pours in from the north, cold air, stacks of it

The room is struck into a green fever
Stained bed, book, scratched windowpane.

A twenty-six-year-old man, plump boy face sets pen to paper—
My birth is my fatal accident, I can never recover from my childhood loneliness.

Dark body once cupped in a mother's arms
Now in a house of dust.

Not cipher, not scheme
For others to throttle and parse

(Those hucksters and swindlers,
Purveyors of hot hate, casting him out).

Seeing stardust, throat first, he leapt
Then hung spread-eagled in air:

The trees of January bore witness.
Did he hear the chirp from a billion light years away,

Perpetual disturbance at the core?
There is a door each soul must go through,

A swinging door—
I have to get seven months of my fellowship,

One lakh and seventy thousand rupees.
Please see to it that my family is paid that.

She comes to him, girl in a cotton sari, holding out both her hands.
Once she loosened her blouse for him

In a garden of milk and sweat,
Where all who are born go down into dark,

Where the arnica, star flower no one planted
Thrives, so too the wild rose and heliotrope.

Her scrap of blue puckers and soars into a flag
As he rappels down the rock face into our lives

We who dare to call him by his name—giddy spirit
Become fire that consumes things both dry and moist,

Ruined wall, grass, river stone,
Thrusts free the winter trees from their own crookedness,

Strikes us from the fierce compact of silence,
Igniting red roots, riotous tongues.

IN MEMORY OF ROHITH VEMULA (1989–2016)

Moksha

At the tail end of the year
Leaving the dry season behind

I saw leaves the color of sparrow's wings
Dissolve into the brickwork of a railway station,

A sudden turn of the head and there she stood
On a dusty platform, wool sweater

Smoldering hair, the familiar heaviness of flesh,
Aged a few years, my sister-in–law

After all the winds of the underworld will do that to you,
By her side a suitcase

Glistening leather bound with straps,
Inside a packet of powdered rice

A morsel of coconut, three red chilies
Fodder for the household gods.

*

Last night in dreams I watched her
In a crush of women severed from their bodies

Drifting as slit silk might
In a slow monsoon wind.

By her, in a kurta knotted at the sleeves
—Who knew that spirits could beckon through clothes—

The one they called Nirbhaya—
A young thing, raped by six men in a moving bus

(She fought back with fists and teeth)
Near Munirka bus station where I once stood

Twenty-three years old, just her age,
Clad in thin cotton, shivering in my sandals.

*

Now I hear them sing
In delicate recitative

My sister-in-law and Nirbhaya,
That other, less than half her age,

A song as intricate as scrimshaw
In vowels that flowered

Before all our tongues began,
Their voices

The color of the bruised
Roses of Delhi.

IN MEMORY OF JYOTI SINGH PANDEY
(1989–2012)

Staggering Skyward

A road without beginning,
Branches of dirt, plumes of mist

A temple squats pink against the sky
A priest in a T-shirt rubs his eyes

Anoints the car, then my forehead—
I have a mark from the goddess of the mountains

It will not wash off easily.
A sedan speeds by, in the window a sign

DANGER, then scrawled under it
BEAUTY NOT MAKE LOVE.

I think I understand this
Imperfectly.

*

A man with a herd of young cows comes close
The cows are reddish colored, burnished.

By the herd, a dressing table
Tossed over the rock's edge

Flimsy wood and metal,
Daubed with paint.

I am entering my own life.
What is inside, what is outside

None of that is clear anymore.
I teeter at the edge of the clouds.

An orange wire dangles at the cliff's edge
VSNL broadband,

Another's stretched taut for birds to hop
Magpies, hummingbirds

Even the purple headed thrush.
Below the dusty road where the tree line parts

Tracks of farmers' feet
Also jackal and snow leopard.

Mountain wild as the sea
Where souls spin and dart.

*

1914, after his student years in the West,
Grandfather scudded home

The boat with his notebooks was torpedoed out of water.
I shut my eyes, catch flecks of fire,

Syllables rubbing against each other
In salt water

Slow pour of sense,
Archive with no place.

*

Something strums in my ear,
A hot wire warbling.

Where is grandfather now?
No birdsong

Just the thud of the car engine
In this high country

As copper melts into rocks
And clouds fashion themselves into palaces

For the wounded,
A sky burial.

*

In Haripur, a girl laughs in a room.
A tree, spectral now,

Her scarlet skirt dangling from a twig
A spurt of the past—

When will this stop?
We are approaching the end of pastoral,

Each rock, each root
Scratched by incipient flame.

The taxi picks up speed.
The driver coughs, starts to question me—

Why go up this mountain?
Wires droop from telegraph poles

And by vaulting rock
Dry grass, slashed at the root

Utterly mute,
Fit for someone's pyre.

No Rescue (with Toy Cars)

You thought that by crossing all these seas
Writing all these poems something would happen.
But nothing has happened except that you have grown
Older; that is one part of it, the other the gods know
But keep quiet about. They hide the secret
In their clenched fists.
Over and over they fold their muslin
Handkerchiefs, the ones used for waving
Good-byes. No amount of saffron or incense
Will make them change their minds.
Nor does the peddler help, he cries out in a hoarse
Voice, old man with rusty bicycle, toy cars tied to the
Handlebars, tiny plastic things in the gray colors
Of the sea gates of your city.

Crossroad

There I am, almost at the crossroad
Stuck in a sudden storm of bikers, men in leather, engines snarling.
Flags spurt skywards.

I freeze at the metal barricade, the seam of sense unpicked,
Brown body splayed.
In the aftermath of light, what proof is there of love—

Buoyancy of the soul hard to mark
Apart from the body
Its tenuous equilibrium unpicked,

Wave after wave of arrival
Etching questions in encircling air
As if life depended on such flammable notations.

*

You come, sari with blue border blowing,
Just as I saw you first, head bare.
A sudden turn on asphalt, you reach out your arms

As if in a palash grove and call to me—
Come over here!
Sometimes the bleeding petals bring down a house

Bring down a republic.
Children are bought and sold for money—
Ghee to burn her. Teen *taka. Ten rupees.* Ek *taka, one rupee.*

Cloth to cover her with.
Camphor for the burning. Bhang to make her drowsy.
Turmeric. Chandan.

You halt at the crossroad, hair thrummed by a savage wind
(Later I try to follow marks of feet, touch cold cotton
That lashed your flesh in place).

*

I hear your voice—
Brood, and it will come, a seizure of sense, a reckoning:
Write with chalk, sticks of lead, anything to hand

Use a bone, a safety pin, a nail, write on paper or stone
Let the poem smolder in memory.
In the desolation of time write

How one inked the bubble with a woman's name
Way at the top of the paper ballot, saw her own hand quiver.
This was in the school with empty metal desks, near Fort Tryon Park.

One set her nipple to her infant's lips
Felt her heart sprout wings, flit over the barbed wire
Of the Immigration Detention Center.

One whimpered in her sleep—Mother, I know I am a tree,
I trail my roots behind me, the man with bad hair will ax me down.
One daubed her face with white paint, crawled

Into a cage outside the museum, hung a sign round
Her own neck—*We are barbarians come to live amongst you,*
Some of us speak this language.

*

Hoarse already, you whisper—
Come closer to me.
You who were born in the Gangetic plains

A year after midcentury
Consider the fragility of the horizon,
The arc of stars into which your father raised you.

When you fall, as surely you will one day
Try to swim forward into blackness
Arms pointing to where you imagine the vault of heaven to be

As Draupadi did, a great throated cry
She made in the forest,
Only the birds could save her, they picked up her cries.

Think of Antigone, who anointed her brother's corpse with dirt
To keep away the wild dogs,
She too made bird sounds, guttural cries.

Go to Standing Rock, where people mass outside their tents
In splintering cold, to guard the quiet springs of water.
There the palash blooms,

Tree used for timber, resin, dye,
Tinting the nails of the love god.
On its leaves names swarm—

Anna Mae Aquash, Eric Garner, Freddie Gray,
Balbir Singh Sodhi, Julia de Burgos countless more.
Thrust from earth's core

From the shadow of musk deer,
The green throat of the hummingbird,
In the honeycomb of light, they step forward to be counted.

IN MEMORY OF MAHASWETA DEVI (1926–2016)

Indian Ocean Blues

LYRIC EGO

Muslin and lavender
Under mosquito nets,
Nothing to hold—just drops of blood
From an ancestral sword.

Grateful acknowledgment is made to the editors of the following journals and anthologies where these poems first appeared:

Academy of American Poets, Poem-A-Day Series: "Night Theater." What Celan said about language in extremity has always haunted me. I was also thinking how we have no words for the act of giving birth. It was important to me that the poet's coat should be green.

Al-Mutanabbi Street Anthology (2012): "Fragment, in Praise of the Book"

Arkansas International: "Chilika Lake"

Black Renaissance/Noire: "Indian Ocean Blues." My thanks to Quincy Troupe, who bore with me patiently as I kept making and remaking this poem, first in New York City, then in the mountains of Shimla. A slightly different version of "Indian Ocean Blues" appeared in *Indian Literature*.

    I had my fifth birthday on the steamer SS *Jehangir*, which was taking us from Bombay to Port Sudan. From the age of five to the age of eighteen (when I left for my studies in England), each year I traveled back and forth across the Indian Ocean. Aimé Césaire's *Cahier d'un retour au pays natal* and his *Corps perdu* have been so powerful for me. Time and again, I could hear the waves beat in his lines. One sea leads to another. In the course of working on my poem I listened to music. Vijay Iyer's *Solo* gave me inspiration, solace, a thread of time to mark my words against. The *Ramayana* story of Sita cast out by her lordly husband Rama (the earth tore open to give her refuge) was something I grew up with. I imagine Sita in the northern reaches of Manhattan. Two words in Malayalam: *udisthanam*—foundation, often used to evoke the sacred; *tarawad*—ancestral house.

Boston Review: "Crossroad." I am grateful to Gayatri Spivak for inviting me to be part of the celebration of Mahasweta Devi, where I was able to read the earliest version of this poem (Columbia University, December 9, 2016). I then read the poem on the steps of New York Public Library as part of the PEN American Center's Writers Resist gathering, January 15, 2017.

Callalloo: "Harlem Cleopatra." This poem was inspired by Roy DeCarava's photograph "Gittel, 1950." It was first published under a different title. My thanks to Sherrie Turner DeCarava, who invited me to compose the poem and take part in a memorial for Roy.

English (U.K.): "Univocity." Scattered pieces of life are crystallized here—grandmother's death before Indian independence, well before I was born; painful memories from childhood; reading Gerard Manley Hopkins a few years later in Khartoum, Sudan; summer in Provincetown, when I saw Robert Motherwell's oil-on-paper series *Beside the Sea*. My thanks to the Norman Mailer Center and Writers Colony, where I was the poetry mentor for the fellows gathered there at the edge of the bay.

Poem (U.K.): "Net Work," "Magnificat"

The Hindu Literary Supplement (December 6, 2014): "Moksha"

India Quarterly: "Aesthetic Knowledge," "Attar," "Bright Passage," "Debt Ridden," "Death of a Young Dalit"

Pen America: "Phyllis Wheatley Suite" under the title "Fear Not: Two for Phillis Wheatley"

Plume Anthology of Poetry, volume 2: "Dreaming in Shimla—Letter to My Mother" under the title "Hard Dreaming"

Solstice: "Little Burnt Holes"

TriQuarterly Review: "The Journey"

Washington Square Review: "Atmospheric Embroidery." The reference in the poem is to Alighiero Boetti's embroidery artwork *I mille fiumi più lunghi del mondo* (*The Thousand Longest Rivers in the World*), 1976–82, exhibited at MOMA in 2012.

Weber—The Contemporary West: An earlier version of "Dreaming in Shimla—Letter to My Mother."

World Literature Today: "Death of a Young Dalit," "Fragments of an Inexistent Whole"

*

Darfur Poems

I spent part of my childhood and teenage years in Sudan and had friends from the Darfur region. These poems were inspired by drawings by children from Darfur who lived in the relief camps on the Chad border. The children used crayons and paper brought by visitors from Human Rights Watch. I am grateful to Steve Crawshaw and Elena Testi of Human Rights Watch for allowing me to work with the drawings stored in New York City. In "Green Leaves of El Fasher," the image of a girl in a pink striped scarf was inspired by a photo by Ron Haviv. The poems themselves were first published in the following journals, my thanks to the editors:

American Poetry Review: "Sand Music," "In Our Lifetime," "Last Colors." Also published in *American Poetry Review*: "Staggering Skywards," "Game of Ghosts"

Fence: "Nurredin," "Child's Notebook" under the title "Darfur Notebook," "There She Stands"

Nimrod: "Green Leaves of El Fasher"

Under the title "Flesh Rose" the Darfur cycle of poems was later published in the *International Literary Quarterly* (London).

"Bright Passage" was composed for the exhibition "Beyond Bollywood: Indian Americans Shape the Nation," held at the Smithsonian in Washington, D.C., 2014–2015. The first stanza of the poem appeared on the wall of the exhibit on the left, just as you entered, above a trunk filled with various articles a migrant might have brought with her.

Grateful acknowledgment to the Indian Institute of Advanced Study, Shimla, for permission to use portions of "Dreaming in Shimla—Letter to My Mother" from my chapbook of the same name (Shimla: Indian Institute of Advanced Study, 2015). Thanks especially to the director, Chetan Singh, who invited me there as a National Fellow.

Namaskars to my wonderful agent Priya Doraswamy, who believes in my work. Special thanks to my fine editor Parneshia Jones who helped shape this collection, and to all at Northwestern University Press for bringing this book to light. Many thanks to friends who supported me in the years it took to make this—some read the poems, others shared a cup of coffee or wine— they and many others not named here helped me through the passages of life: Andrea Belag, Anita Desai, Jesseca Ferguson, Marilyn Hacker, Kimiko Hahn, Githa Hariharan, Zarina Hashmi, Svati Joshi, Wallis Wilde Menozzi, Grace Schulman, Leah Souffrant, Sarah Van Arsdale, Gauri Viswanathan, Monika Weiss, Ronaldo Wilson. Thanks to my cousin Verghis Koshi and to my brother-in-law Joe Lelyveld and Janny Scott. I could not have done this without the love of David Lelyveld, my fellow traveler, and our new generation—Adam Kuruvilla Lelyveld and Svati Mariam Lelyveld.